The Flag
of
Yoshiharu

The Flag

of

Yoshiharu

Yvonne Boisclaire

The Flag of Yoshiharu

©1996 by Yvonne Boisclaire

Clearwood Publishers
P.O. Box 52
Bella Vista, California 96008

First Edition, 1996
Printed in the United States of America

Library of Congress Card Number 96-85956
ISBN 0-9649997-1-4

Photo Credits:
Hideo Tsunoi, Yokosuka, Japan
Kiyotaka Shishido, Sendai, Japan
Aoki Susumu, Kamakura Shinbun, Yokosuka, Japan
Kumi Ushida, Sankai Press, Yokosuka, Japan
Jesse Campbell, Anderson, California
Larry and Yvonne Boisclaire

Art: Ruth Nakatani
Cover design: Cheri McKinzie

Acknowledgments

I wish to extend my gratitude to the following people who made this book possible:

Jesse Campbell for the gift of the Japanese war flag;

Andrew Gebert for his interpretation of the flag and his hand in making our journey to Japan possible;

Shinichi Nishimura for locating the family of Yoshiharu;

The Tsunoi family for allowing publication of their story;

Kiyotaka Shishido for photography;

Kumi Shishido and Aoki Susumu for press coverage;

Michio Takenaka, Takao Takahashi, and YWAM, Takatsuki, for consultation in Japan;

Kyoko Hara Amero for consultation in the U.S.;

George Gunn, Lynn Doiron, Christine Cicero (CT Publishing), Glenn Hassenpflug, and my daughter, Yvette Boisclaire, for editing;

Troy Reimers for layout;

Brett Larsen and Dennis David for computer support;

My sister, Marlys Carusone, my parents, Jim and Renee Miller; and my friends Ruth Nakatani, Richard Mills, and Bonnie Hansen for encouragement;

My husband, Larry Boisclaire, for standing beside me each step of the way on our journey to Japan and for his invaluable work in editing and producing this book.

Yvonne Boisclaire

Preface

The Man Yoshiharu Tsunoi

Contrary to popular assessments in the present day western world, not all men are motivated soley by consumption, greed, sensuality, and individual rights.

Some men regard the needs of others as more important than their own. They reach out to embrace a widening circle of care: family and friends; neighbors and local community; nation or groups of nations, including the global human population; the environs of the earth, its flora and fauna; and the spiritual realm encompassing our planet.

These noble ones are disciples of higher laws: truth, honor, loyalty to duty, faith, hope, and love. The glitter of money, power, and materialism cannot lure the trancendent man away from the principles that guide his path.

Yoshiharu Tsunoi followed this course. He was a lover of beauty and people—a teacher, a man who knew himself and the meaning of life.

Looking back on his life before 1945, we detect actions that bespeak of strong ideals. Among these faith stands out. Faith stirred Yoshiharu to leave behind a momento containing his secret message. Through it he revealed the reason for his lifestyle. He believed his message would be delivered at the appropriate time, even though he would not likely be alive to see it happen. For faith is the acting upon one's belief in advance of witnessing the results.

It is hoped this narrative will serve as an inspiration for all men and women to reach for the higher laws. In so doing we might preserve this planet called earth and its populace.

Larry Boisclaire

Table of Contents

荆心雪

Can any good thing arise
  From the ashes of Mount Samat—
That mosquito-plagued plot of land
  Stained with the blood of young men?

A hard, malevolent land
  Of jungle, vine, viper, and swamp.
Sultry, hot, musty, rank,
  A land that befriends no man.

Listen, can you hear them;
  Can you hear the youths cry out?
Sick, hungry, aching, beaten,
  Alone in this hostile land.

Japan, America, Philippines
  It matters not what nation—
The insatiable reaper, the reaper of war,
  Cut down our favorite sons.

The Flag of Yoshiharu
is dedicated to all who suffered or died
during the Great War.

義沼不無為候ゝ才衰にきせ二よ

Prologue

August 9th

The Boeing 737 soars through the clear skies of northern Oregon at 31,000 feet. Dim at first, then unmistakable, the landmarks of Seattle come into our view.

To the northeast appears the wrinkled face of Mount Rainier, rising steadfast above the valleys and foothills of Washington. Directly below, the gray outline of the mighty Columbia River snakes east to separate Washington from Oregon.

I stand up briefly for a peek west and see what I expect—the shimmering Pacific Ocean, stretching for endless miles beyond our left wing.

Ever so subtly the airship dips her wings. Could it be a salute to her birthplace, the Boeing mega-plant far below?

World War II is on my mind. I touch the familiar arm beside me and whisper our location to my husband, Larry. What will transpire on our mission is uncertain. But this I know: it is August 9, a memorable day in history. The river snaking below us played its part in the drama many years ago.

Along that river, in the eastern plains of Washington, scientists of a previous era harnessed the frigid waters of the powerful Columbia to cool a nuclear reactor and give birth to plutonium. They produced the radioactive element to arm a bomb named Fat Man.

Fifty years ago today, on August 9, 1945, a Boeing B-29 bomber cruised over Japan at 31,000 feet and sent Fat Man to its target—Nagasaki. The devastation it produced hastened the end of the war.

The Boeing we fly in carries no warhead. Instead, it carries a flag, concealed from the pilot, the crew, and the passengers who sip cold drinks and munch peanuts. I am wearing the flag in the safest place I could find—tucked inside a sash encircling my waist. The flag once belonged to a Japanese soldier, Yoshiharu Tsunoi. Having been in exile for fifty-one years, the flag will return to its homeland today.

The jet from San Francisco begins its descent into British Columbia. Vancouver Island stretches out to the west, a tree-clad land mass rising from the sea. Beneath our flight path lie the beautiful San Juan Islands—hidden from us but pleasant to behold, like jewels cast upon the emerald sea.

The Boeing sets down at Vancouver, Canada, completing the first leg of our journey. We board another Boeing, a magnificent 747, for our flight to Japan. Soon, she rises like a graceful bird, then swings over the steep coastal mountains of British Columbia and heads across the

Pacific Ocean.

Nine hours after departure the Boeing sets down at Narita International Airport. We take a train to Tokyo Station, and here we meet Andrew Gebert for the first time. The young American approaches us, smiling. He queries with an accented, "Yvonne, Larry?" and offers his hand in greeting. It seems as if we know Andrew already. We have communicated by telephone several times before today. Andrew is an interpreter from New York City.

Our new friend hails a taxi. As we dart through Tokyo's narrow streets, Andrew talks fluently, first in English, then in Japanese, switching with ease as he speaks to us and the driver in turn. We like him already. He delivers us safely to our hotel and bids us goodnight. Larry and I will spend the night on the ninth floor of the Ochiyanomizuin, resting for the appointed day on the morrow.

Moat surrounding the Imperial Palace
(Boisclaire)

Chapter 1

The Homecoming

The day of presentation arrives, August 11 in Japan. We lost August 10 while flying over the International Date Line.

Larry and I venture from our hotel at six in the morning to discover a sleepy Tokyo of deserted streets and closed shops. We expected Tokyo to be alive twenty-four hours a day.

We wander a mile or so through a network of streets until we reach the moat surrounding the Imperial Palace. An envoy, in the form of a white swan, comes out to greet us. He cuts a path through the murky gray-green water and inquires as to our purpose. Since we have no food, he loses interest and swims away.

Checking his watch, Larry heads us back. Negotiating Tokyo proves to be taxing. We cannot speak or read any Japanese, and every block looks like the previous one.

As we make our way through the maze, the sleeping giant of Tokyo begins to rouse—delicious aromas waft from the small cafes along the way; people, cars, and buses fill the streets. We do not tarry in the burgeoning crowd. Andrew Gebert will come for us soon.

We diligently retrace our steps: one block east, six blocks north, scurry along a few more blocks, walk under a bridge and up a staircase to successfully reach our hotel.

Back in our room we change—a gray suit for Larry, a pink floral outfit for me. Now my attention goes to the flag, still hidden in the sash. I sigh with relief, *At last, it is safe in Japan.* For the past year I have stored the flag in a safe-deposit box. During our voyage, I secured the flag to my person, unwilling to trust such a prize to luggage or even my purse. Luggage can be lost and purses snatched.

Now I spread the flag out on the bed and smooth the creases. I stand back for one last look. The flag will soon pass out of my hands.

Time has left little indication of where the flag has been—a dark red stain here, a frayed corner there. *Not bad for fifty-one years,* I muse. Kanji, the written form of Japanese, marches across white silk in rows, artfully enclosing a brilliant Rising Sun. These strange inscriptions provided the road map that led us to Japan. We followed this map so we could return the flag to family and homeland—a final remembrance of a deceased Japanese soldier. On the flag is written his name, Yoshiharu Tsunoi, and the name of his hometown, Takeyama.

I fold the flag gently, wrap it in a square of red silk, and place it in a red photo frame box. The result is striking. A photograph of the flag graces the lid, tucked under glass and edged in black.

Around the box I apply the final wrap, a black cloth, using a Japanese style of wrapping gifts, folded carefully and tied at the top.

Finally, I check my own image in the long mirror behind our door. *Not bad for fifty-one years,* I reflect. I place a necklace around my neck; jet-black to match the bundle I will carry. We gather our baggage and descend by elevator to the lobby.

Andrew arrives with a smiling young Japanese man beside him. Shinichi Nishimura of Tokyo is introduced as Shin, a writer and our guide for today. Shin and Andrew made possible today's event, the return of the flag. Andrew interpreted the Kanji writing on the flag. Shin, in turn, located the surviving brother of Yoshiharu Tsunoi: Hideo Tsunoi.

Wasting no time, the men volunteer to help with our luggage. We obviously overpacked. Loaded down with suitcases, they lead us two blocks down the busy street, and we enter an underground world of subways and trains. Here another joins us—Kiyotaka Shishido, a professional photographer from Sendai. Andrew introduces the gentleman as Kiyo. Together—four men, one woman, one flag, assorted baggage and camera—we make our way through the crowd.

I relish our passage through the subterranian labyrinth.

Behind, in front, and surrounding me on all sides walks the entourage of men. I fancy them to be bodyguards. Andrew Gebert—the American—walks free, easy, and relaxed with a smile on his face. Kiyotaka Shishido—robust, confident, and strong—strides forward with his camera and my suitcase. The young, wiry Shinichi Nishimura—nervous, capable, and frowning—takes his job seriously, determined to get us on the right train. Larry Boisclaire—my partner for life—walks by my side with a bag in each hand.

We have one mind, like a team of couriers bent on the task of delivering a secret document. They carry the luggage; I concentrate my effort on the flag.

As we make our way through the crowd, I become acutely aware of my foreignness. It's not my small size: most of the dark-haired Orientals I see are nearly as short as I am. Rather, my fair features mark me as a stranger in Japan. I'm the only blond in sight. Driven by curiosity, people steal a look, then avert their eyes and hurry past.

None of the people we pass know of the valued object we transport. I clutch the small black bundle to my waist, confident that the flag of Yoshiharu Tsunoi will arrive safely in the hands of the younger brother, who survived the war and fifty ensuing years.

Shinichi stops to labor over a complex list of numbers and strange looking marks—a train schedule. Above the din of trains and hawkers we hear an announcer who delivers a staccato of destinations: "Shinagawa, Yokohama, Chigasaki, Odawara, Yokosuka."

Shin speeds our pace. My shoes click on the tiled floor. We hop a fast train to Yokosuka. Once aboard we choose seats along the padded benches that line the outside walls of the train. I sit between Andrew and Larry. Shin and Kiyo take seats along the opposite side of the car.

The train bolts past a blur of peaked tile roofs, minuscule rice fields, verdant hillocks, minivans and compact trucks, and small excavators that remind me of Tonka toys and bear the names of Fumatsu, Hitachi, or CAT.

"Click-clack, click-clack," Larry on my left, Andrew on my right, we stare at the black-shrouded box resting in my lap and talk of the flag.

From across the aisle Kiyo snaps us with his camera. Shin dozes. We nearly miss our stop, but a startled Shin jerks to life and hustles us off the train.

I step off behind Andrew and notice dark streaks down the back of his cotton shirt. He wipes his forehead and says, "Whew, summer in Yokosuka. It's always like this, hot and humid."

I see nothing special about this place. A station, people milling about, a taxi or two, and the bright green public telephones that seem to be ubiquitous in Japan. It is close to midday and much hotter now than when we started south two hours ago. The humidity must be hovering near 95 percent.

Out of the crowd steps a gray-haired man of medium build. He introduces himself to Andrew as Hideo Tsunoi, shakes Andrew's hand, then pulls a small towel from his pocket and mops pearls of sweat from his head, face, arms, and the open neck of his shirt. I notice the pink floral pattern of his shirt—same color as my jacket. He smiles but seems unsure, perhaps nervous. Then, with the manners of a perfect gentleman, he nods and offers his hand to Shin, Kiyo, and Larry. Lastly, Mr. Tsunoi offers his hand to me. He says, "Ah, E-Von."

A young man joins our group. Tsunoi introduces the handsome youth as his son, Kiyokazu. He has come to help transport us. The Tsunoi men take up our suitcases and lead us to their waiting cars, then whisk us away in a motorcade of two cars: interpreter, writer, photographer, husband, wife, luggage, and flag.

Mr. Tsunoi seems absorbed in thought. No one mentions the flag. Only small talk transpires as we wind our way to Yokosuka. We pass gardens, houses, and Tonka-like excavators. After fifteen minutes, Mr. Tsunoi pulls a hard right and enters a narrow drive.

The driveway leads into a clearing bordered by lush trees and dense shrubbery. Thick bamboo stalks shoot thirty feet skyward through a canopy of vine-draped trees. Even at this moment, workmen hack at the tall grass and shrubs. We are witnessing an incessant battle between man and flora.

We ease to a stop in the sunny clearing. A white two-story house stands before us. I notice an older structure— dark, wooden, and weather-beaten—fifty yards away, tucked against the bamboo forest.

As we step out of Mr. Tsunoi's air-conditioned car a blast of hot air confronts us. Even more surprising is the jungle's pulsating din of buzz, croak, click, hum. A million unseen insects compete for food, mates, or territory—I do not know which, but I can almost feel them crawling on my skin. I stare at the jungle, fascinated.

The second car arrives. Andrew, Shin, and Kiyo seem oblivious to the shrill racket that has me riveted to the spot. Mrs. Tsunoi rushes from the white house to greet us. She's stocky, appears to be in her early sixties, and has tied her beautiful, long, gray-streaked black hair into a ponytail.

Tsunoi san (Mr. Tsunoi) introduces his wife as Atsuko. I want to imprint this day on my brain—the words spoken, the emotions felt, all the details around us. But I am finding it hard to wrench my attention from the bugs. Atsuko finds it hard to convey her feelings by spoken word. She grasps our hands. The moistness of her eyes reveals unspoken emotions.

Tsunoi san ushers us inside. Like a lead curtain slammed shut, the front door cuts off the dripping hot air and cacophony outside. It's cool and quiet in here. A step is located five feet inside the door, and a tub has been placed there. It holds ice and a bounty of American drinks: Budweiser, Pepsi, Bartles and Jaymes, and Welch's. An array of footwear lies at the bottom and top of the step. I have never entered a Japanese home before today, but I follow the expected custom and remove my shoes. We select our drinks, then add five more pairs of shoes to the collection and step up into the living room.

A large table with short legs fills any walking space the room may have had. Trays of sushi and other Japanese food, along with egg sandwiches, apple pie, and an unlikely but colorful punch made of fruit cocktail and Jell-O cubes crowd the table's lace-covered surface. Cushions circle the perimeter, and for any who prefer, including *gaijin* (foreigners), a sofa sits nearby. A fan whirs in the corner. I'm glad for the drink, I'm glad for the fan, I'm glad to be rid of my shoes, and I wiggle my nyloned toes in the soft carpet.

The young man Kiyokazu hurries off to work, but Tsunoi's lovely teenage daughter, Yoshimi, greets us. She and Atsuko make sure everyone is comfortable and properly supplied with drinks.

As we settle in, a conversation catches my attention. I hear Tsunoi san speak my name. When I look across the room, I see him mop his face for the twelfth time and stuff the already wet towel down his shirt. He has spoken his wish to Andrew in a soft but resolute voice. "Can E-Von show me the flag?"

They look over at me, and I answer, "Yes, that would be fine."

We move into the adjoining room, small and cube-shaped, having a special floor covering of woven straw, called tatami. Like a typical tatami room, this one is barren of furniture except for one low table. The far wall is decorated with a scroll and other Japanese objects of art, with a religious alcove, called *tokonoma,* in the corner. A Buddhist altar is the focal point. Two round watermelons rest on a low shelf beneath the altar. I notice a small statue of Buddha and an incense burner on the shelf below. Larry and I are Christians. How different this *tokonoma* seems from our place of worship back home. Then I see a bottle of juice and cups beside the altar. They remind me of our own observance of communion.

Two vases of flowers adorn the altar. I wonder if this is for today's occasion. Not only has the flag come home, but it's mid-August. This week, Buddhists throughout Japan celebrate O Bon, a festival for the dead. According to their beliefs, the spirits of ancestors return to earth during this time.

Tsunoi san and I kneel facing one another. I place the black bundle between us and look up at Kiyo. Satisfied his camera is ready, I press my gift toward Hideo Tsunoi and say, "I present you with the flag of Yoshiharu Tsunoi."

Cameras click. Tsunoi san unwraps the black cloth, opens the box, and lifts out the flag in its red silk wrapper. He says, "Oh, red." Then he unfolds the silk to find his brother's long-lost flag. Now he is speechless. He reverently spreads Yoshiharu's flag between us.

I have seen it many times before. I've touched the smooth weave of white silk and gazed at the brilliant red globe. I've traced the black lines with my eyes and wondered at their meaning. A strange sensation stirs within me, and I am drawn for another look, just like the first time, the second time, and now what may be the last time.

Tsunoi san, too, leans forward, inspecting for the first time in fifty-one years the flag his brother carried off to war. Surely this flag must have special significance.

For a small space in time, Tsunoi san and I are motionless. I am happy for him but sad for me. I will not be touching the flag again. My year of custodial care has come and gone.

Tsunoi san scratches his head. He must be reading his brother's name. I wonder what he is thinking. It is difficult to imagine him fifty years ago as a child, Yoshiharu's younger brother, Hideo. It's equally difficult to reckon with my presence here, seated on tatami. Little did I imagine, just a few months ago, where the red and white cloth would lead.

Left to right: Andrew, Yvonne, and Larry
on train to Yokosuka (Shishido)

Atsuko Tsunoi greeting the Boisclaires (Shishido)

Passing of the flag to Hideo Tsunoi *(Boisclaire)*

"Oh, red," says Hideo *(Boisclaire)*

Chapter 2

The Flag

ℐ first saw the flag in a photograph belonging to Jesse Campbell. It was mid-August 1994, the season I would later come to know as O Bon.

Jesse became a heart patient that year, and I was his nurse. As a registered nurse at Redding Medical Center, I teach cardiac rehabilitation to patients such as Jesse. Our rehab team provides exercise tutelage on an outpatient basis.

Usually, our participants come from wide and varied backgrounds. The particular class I found Jesse in was made up of eight U.S. veterans—WWII, Korean War, and Vietnam era veterans.

Although veterans are plentiful in our northern California area, I had never known of a class composed exclusively of veterans. Every day they talked of war: duty at sea, duty on land, the jungle, the food, the mud, the adventure and hardship they'd borne. Next thing I knew, they began bringing in old photographs to share.

In Jesse Campbell's album, I spotted a photograph with two young American soldiers wearing Japanese flags wrapped around their waists. I asked Jesse to explain it.

Jesse said, "This handsome young fellow is me, that one is my buddy. We found the flags on Bataan at the end of WWII. Japanese soldiers carried them for good luck." Then he added, "I still have mine to this day."

I had to see that flag.

For the past six months, I had nurtured a strong interest in the war of the Philippines. So much so, I had begun writing a true story of an American POW who was captured on Bataan. I knew our soldiers had surrendered and became prisoners of the Japanese in 1942. Jesse Campbell's outfit, the 38th Division of the U.S. Army, known as the *Avengers of Bataan,* helped liberate the Philippines in 1945.

Jesse agreed to bring his flag to class. When he did, I sensed the significance of the old war flag—carried to Bataan by a Japanese soldier, who, in the end, tasted defeat and death. With Jesse's permission, I took the flag home and clicked off three rolls of film before returning it at our next Cardiac Rehab session.

Two weeks later, on the occasion of my birthday, Jesse pressed an envelope into my hands. "It's for you," he said.

I looked inside and could not believe what I saw—the Rising Sun! At first I declined the valuable gift. But Jesse persisted with, "I've had the flag fifty years. Now you keep it."

So it was that the flag passed from Yoshiharu to Jesse to Yvonne. Now I have passed it on to the final caretaker, Hideo. We are still kneeling on tatami. After a respectful pause, I ask Hideo if he remembers the day Yoshiharu received the flag.

"Yes," replies Hideo in perfect English. "I was ten years old. It happened behind the old house. We had a banzai.

Jesse passes the flag *(Boisclaire)*

Hideo Tsunoi with his brother's flag *(Boisclaire)*

Chapter 3

Banzai

Hideo lets his mind wander back to mid-August 1944, during the week of O Bon. He relates the story of a banzai ceremony held in Takeyama, Japan.

"Yoshiharu was an artist. He did not go to war at first. Not strong but physically weak, he had a low ranking in the army. Finally, they drafted him.

"We had a banzai. It's a send-off party where everyone comes to wish the departing soldier good luck. We should have been exuberant. With Yoshiharu, we felt gloomy. He was not a soldier at heart, and we doubted we would ever see him again.

"We gathered in front of the old house, fifty people in all. My father, Shigeji Tsunoi, held up Yoshiharu's flag. 'Banzai, Banzai, Banzai.' The guests raised their hands in the air three times and shouted the slogan, meaning, 'Hurrah, hurrah, cheers for a long life.'

"Yoshiharu smiled and turned to his father beside him. Those standing nearby may have seen a hint of tears in Father's eyes. He feared this to be his last day with his son, my brother.

"Yoshiharu seemed happy. What more could a man want than to be honored by those he loved? He had loyal friends and family and now a good luck flag. But the moment would pass quickly, then he must head off to war.

"Beneath the smile, Yoshiharu's heart grieved. We knew, he knew, but everyone pretended. No doubt he had considered his lot. Each time he had, he could only return to the facts: when a man went to war, he did not come back.

"Yoshiharu numbered his days and used them wisely. During the previous week he spent time to dote on each of us: our sisters, Saku, Kiku, Sayo, and Tatsuko, and myself. Even our oldest brother, Takataroh, had come home from Tokyo to say goodbye.

"I saw Yoshiharu pass graciously among the guests. He walked from one man to the next, using the moment to grasp one, nod at another, and exchange a last farewell with yet another. Finally, the shadows of the day lengthened, and the guests began to disperse. They left one by one, walking down the road that led away from our house."

Hideo pauses. Sensing the break, Atsuko calls us into the living room to eat. We begin to feast on Japanese delectables.

I gaze at the food. It's more than eight people can eat. Suddenly I'm hungry, and I fill my plate. My mouth savors each delicious bite, but my mind cannot pull away from the banzai, fifty-one years ago, possibly to the day.

Yoshiharu's family most likely had a big spread that day. It would have been a hardship on the family during those lean times. By 1944 everyone felt the war. . .

Nearly every family in Japan had suffered loss of a loved one or property. Most would have had banzai parties, and most would have said goodbye to father or son or both. Cities had been destroyed by bombings, families disrupted, schools suspended, and women compelled to work.

Individuals were of no concern to Imperial General Headquarters. Japan fought a war and urgently needed men. More hardship and suffering loomed ahead. Unknown to civilians, the war was not going according to plan. Military leaders conspired to conceal the fact that Japan was losing. In a desperate attempt to salvage their dying cause, the zealous strategists would send yet another wave of men to war.

The draft stretched its ugly tentacles to grasp those previously considered too young, too old, or unfit. It reached out along the Miura Peninsula to a little village called Takeyama. It found thirty-one-year-old Yoshiharu Tsunoi, son of Shigeji and Hisa.

Yoshiharu Tsunoi
circa 1944
(Courtesy of Tsunoi)

Small talk over lunch; left to right, Yvonne, Hideo, Atsuko, and Yoshimi *(Shishido)*

Chapter 4

Benjiroh's Line

We sit back, happy, relaxed, and satiated. We made a fair dent in the food, but the table is still laden. Hideo invites us outdoors. Larry, Andrew, Shin, Kiyo, and I accept. Outside, the clamorous buzzing of insects pervades the air. Hideo says, "Those are cicadae. In summertime we have them all over Japan. Males make that sound to attract females."

Hideo makes a sweeping gesture with his arm and says, "My family has lived here for the past four hundred and fifty years. Today this area is part of Yokosuka. Before the war we had our separate village called Takeyama."

He leads and we amble over to the other structure—
old, dark, weathered. Hideo unlocks the door and announces, "My grandfather Benjiroh Tsunoi built this house
in 1886. It was known as the Benjiroh House. Yoshiharu
lived on the second floor. Atsuko and I built the new house
six years ago."

The old house is of traditional Japanese style, having
tatami floors, screen dividers, and large hardwood beams,
blackened with age. As we walk through the Benjiroh House,
Hideo continues talking. It is easy to weave a story: an active
family, a working farm, a place called Takeyama, and a time
in history during the flip side of our century.

The ancient land we call Japan is neatly divided into
districts and prefectures. Tokyo lies in the Kanto district.
Fifty miles south of Tokyo, in the Kanagawa prefecture, a
mass of land juts into the Pacific Ocean to form the western shore of Tokyo Bay—the Miura Peninsula.

Shaped surprisingly like the boot of Italy, this crooked
thumb of land boasts a climate of its own. Mountains to the
west stop the howling winter air from reaching Miura
shores. The mild Pacific current swirls on three sides to temp-
er the climate even more. Summers wax hot and humid.

As in most of Japan, mountainous terrain character-
izes the peninsula, leaving but a scant allotment of habitable land. Dense thickets of vines, trees, and bamboo choke
the land, encouraged ever thicker by rich soils and gener-
ous rains.

Tucked between the mountains and hills, pockets of
fertile land yield abundant crops. For centuries, these tiny
parcels have passed from one generation to the next. The
ancient Tsunoi family farmed here, on a piece of land in
the village of Takeyama.

Tsunois of today can trace their family lines back four
hundred fifty years on the same plot. Shigeji Tsunoi was

the last in his line to till the fertile soil. He and his wife, Hisa, worked the family land in the early 1900's, just as their forebears had done for the past four centuries.

Behind the large house, a rice terrace had been chiseled into the gently sloping land. An ancient artesian well provided water to flood the rice. Year-round seasonal rains lavishly watered the fruits and vegetables. Everything flourished, including the prized cherry trees and the native vegetation surrounding the house.

Even the people flourished. Shigeji Tsunoi cut a well-known image in his community. A dedicated leader, he served his townspeople well. He promoted social welfare, fire prevention, and the improvement of agricultural techniques. He held office on the school board and performed shrine and temple duty. All this he accomplished, in addition to running a farm.

Tsunoi family mark, used for labelling
produce containers for shipping

As if to compete with the fertile soil, Shigeji and Hisa brought forth children liberally, eleven in all. Eight survived childhood: three males born in succession—Takataroh, Shohzoh, Yoshiharu; then four females—Saku, Kiku, Sayo, Tatsuko. Last born was Hideo, a boy. Twenty-three years separated the oldest and youngest, with hardly time between to wean and raise the little ones. The sturdy farmer loved each of his offspring, from Takataroh, the oldest, to little Hideo, the baby.

Raising eight children on a farm meant rice to plant,

vegetables to tend, weeds to pull, animals to care for, and a hundred other activities to provide a steady flow of food and clothing and necessities. It could not have been an idle life. Shigeji nurtured the land and the little Tsunois while at the same time subduing the elements, particularly the vigorous bamboo forest pressing in upon the family's habitable area.

The cataclysmic forces of nature cannot be controlled. In 1923 a devastating earthquake rocked the Kanto area. It hit Tokyo hard. The quake and its aftermath of fires left hundreds and thousands dead and homeless. In Takeyama it knocked the Benjiroh House flat, but no one was hurt. A determined Shigeji rebuilt the house with the same materials, including the heavy hardwood beams erected by his father.

During Shigeji's reign there were few cars or phones in Japan. This did not stop Takeyama's folk from keeping in close contact. Like a tangle of neurons connecting vital parts of the brain, roads and pathways connected the scattered families. The narrow lanes ambled between low hills to connect farm to house to marketplace.

Leading us from the old house, Hideo points down an abandoned track that disappears into the jungle and says, "This road led to our house."

Before Hideo can say more, Andrew looks at his watch and informs everyone that he and his friends must catch a train to Tokyo. We all shake hands and say goodbye. Andrew hugs me. Quickly, the trio of men piles into a car and departs, with Hideo's daughter Yoshimi serving as their driver.

I peer down the old route and look up into the tall bamboo. Some stalks are as thick as my leg. A musty jungle smell of mold and rotting leaves fills the air. The sound of cicadae is near. I picture this road following heavy rains.

It would surely become a muddy bog. Nevertheless, people came. They came to the Tsunoi farm in their wagons or on foot. They came to trade, visit, or consult the respected Shigeji. Later, they would come to see his son Yoshiharu Tsunoi.

Larry and I slowly follow Hideo back to the new house. We join Atsuko inside. Hideo brings out a tattered folder holding Yoshiharu's artwork and photographs. We see Yoshiharu posing at a flower show, dressed in a kimono and robe. We see his *ikebana* sketches, his calligraphy workbook, a portrait of himself and one of his grandmother. Next, we uncover a drawing I recognize—Jesus praying in the Garden of Gethsemane.

I point to the last one and ask Hideo, "Was Yoshiharu a Christian?"

"No, Buddhist," he replies quickly.

And Hideo continues the story.

Yoshiharu at a flower show *(Courtesy of Tsunoi)*

Bamboo forest on Tsunoi grounds *(Shishido)*

Chapter 5

Yoshiharu

"Yoshiharu was born in 1914, the third son of my parents, Shigeji and Hisa. He differed from his older brothers. Not strong, a weak and sickly child from birth, he gravitated toward beauty.

"From a young age, Yoshiharu practiced the arts. He studied drawing, music, and calligraphy. More than anything, he loved *ikebana*, the art of floral arrangement.

"Yoshiharu grew up with a balanced personality; mostly outgoing but at times reserved. My peaceable brother enjoyed people as much as nature. He would drop his work to greet any neighbors who ventured down the dirt road, always ready with a genuine smile. He had a studious side and would lapse into deep concentration for hours. Just as often his light side took over, resulting in boisterous teasing and bouts of laughter."

Hideo goes on to describe Yoshiharu as standing five foot three at maturity, about average for Japanese males of his time. A careful scrutiny of the photographs tells me even more. There was nothing ordinary about the young Tsunoi. He wore his thick black hair longer than the short style of the day. His face looked serious but gentle; not the stern, harsh look of many Japanese men. He wore black-rimmed glasses and a watch. He sometimes appeared in a western-style suit and tie, with fountain pens tucked in the pocket. At another time he appeared in his black silk kimono. All this makes me wonder, *Could any who knew him predict Yoshiharu?* It appears he was an individualist in a country of conformists.

Now I am studying a photograph of Yoshiharu standing in front of several flower arrangements. "A flower show?" I ask.

"Yes," replies Hideo. "Though talented in all the arts, he excelled in *ikebana*. This became his first love. Yoshiharu's gifted hands worked with sprigs of foliage, twisted stems or sticks, dried pods, and touches of colorful flowers. He bent them to his will, yielding striking displays of natural beauty, which greatly pleased his instructor, Kunka Kato.

"The craft offered opportunity for travel. By the time he reached twenty-five, Yoshiharu had mastered *Ikenobo*, a special school of *ikebana*. He attended flower shows in Yokohama and Tokyo. His name placard was displayed with his work. At shows with students, his work was placed in the foremost position in the center of the back row. As a master, he opened the Benjiroh House to teach *ikebana*. He had many students. One was Masuko Sakai."

I am beginning to have a better understanding of the

young Yoshiharu. He cultivated his mind and creativity to overcome physical limitations and grew to be an extraordinary young man. Without doubt, he surpassed any expectations that might have been held for male members of Benjiroh's line.

When not engaged in teaching, farming, or other activities, Yoshiharu would retire to his upstairs room. From his lookout he could oversee the rice and view the tall bamboo shooting skyward. He could hear the buzz of the jungle, vibrant and alive. He could see people walking down the shadowy road. He could watch for Masuko Sakai.

Hideo had described Masuko as much more than a student of Yoshiharu's. They had fallen in love and were engaged to be married. They postponed marriage, not wanting to start a family during the perilous days of war. Yoshiharu and Masuko hoped for war to pass and stable times to come.

Even stable times were not easy in Japan. Japan's masses of suppressed people had been exploited by their rulers since time immemorial. The multitude of tireless workers had supplied cheap labor to feed the rapid industrial growth of the twentieth century and make a few families rich.

But the 1930s and 1940s had transformed life for all people of Japan. Peacetime economy gave way to war. It would be the people who lost again; who fueled the military aggression with their lives and livelihoods. Women, children, and old men toiled to provide war material. Draft-age men fought on foreign shores.

In 1941 tragedy struck the Benjiroh House. Hisa died, leaving Shigeji bereft of his wife and the large family without a mother. Yoshiharu did his utmost to provide love and care for his siblings. For his youngest sister, Tatsuko, he bought a beautiful silk kimono to wear as she mourned for her mother—a priceless gift she never forgot.

Japan, meanwhile, threw all its resources into the war. Food, clothing, medicine, guns, and ammunition followed soldiers to the outermost reaches of the expanding empire, causing supplies to diminish at home.

The war stretched the Tsunoi family thin. The oldest son of the family, Takataroh, had managed Koa Grinder, a machine shop in Tokyo. Once WWII started, hardly a shop or factory continued to operate except for war purposes. Koa now ground gun barrels to satisfy the warmongers. Takataroh continued to manage the shop—probably the only way he avoided the draft. The second son, Shohzoh, was drafted and sent to Sumatra.

This left Yoshiharu next in line. His poor health gave him a low ranking in the Army. At home he ranked high, for in Japan, the eldest son living at home inherits the family house. Along with the inheritance comes responsibility. The heir-apparent assumes more work as his parents age: maintaining the home and farm, tending the family altar, and ultimately caring for the old couple. This mapped Yoshiharu's future. For the time being he continued under his father's authority and worked the family farm.

Farmers had certain advantages. They had plenty to eat and often had surpluses to barter with. The Tsunois managed well. They traded their rice and vegetables for clothing and other goods. For the needy, they generously gave of the excess. Yoshiharu continued to teach, and students continued to negotiate the tangle of roads to reach the large house in the trees.

Yoshiharu led a full life. At night he taught calligraphy at Yokosuka Industrial High School. He was periodically called upon to draw lifelike funeral portraits for his neighbors. The framed portraits were set in the family altar to honor the deceased. As time permitted, he retreated upstairs to play his flute or violin. A busy man, the third son of Tsunoi, he farmed and practiced art. He served his townspeople well. They, in turn, felt proud to claim Yoshiharu as one of their own.

By 1944, at thirty-one, he was a master of *ikebana* and a beloved member of the community of Takeyama.

Yoshiharu with students *(Courtesy of Tsunoi)*

Yoshiharu in western suit *(Courtesy of Tsunoi)*

Sample from Yoshiharu's calligraphy workbook *(Ushida)*

Yoshiharu's placard *(Ushida)*

Chapter 6

The Send-Off

The day intrigues me—the banzai day, fifty-one years ago. Sad goodbyes. Hidden tears. I try to imagine how Yoshiharu and his family must have felt. I ask Hideo if Yoshiharu seemed upset.

"No," replies Hideo. "In his optimistic manner, Yoshiharu told us, 'Don't worry, I'll be back.' We put smiles on our faces, but we had grave doubts. Though not a funeral, the feeling was so. My sisters and I supposed we would never see him again. The neighbors felt the same."

The day descended like a thief, the sad day that stole Yoshiharu from his family and friends. Fifty people had gathered that day. The incongruity of sending Yoshiharu to war would have been conspicuously clear. Those present knew Yoshiharu as a peace-loving man. That, along with poor health, sealed his fate—he would not survive. It grieved them to see the young artisan snatched away for war.

But Japanese citizens of 1944 did not defy authority. Nor did they doubt the nobility of war. For them, loyalty to authority was a given part of life. Fighting for one's country was a privilege. Those who died in battle brought honor to their families and reaped the promise of eternal rewards. The flag shows it. Its writings include slogans of the day: "With Determination for Certain Victory," "Promote the Imperial Cause," "Seven Lives Given to Requite One's Debt of Gratitude to Sovereign and Country,"and "Yoshiharu, Live for the Grand and Eternal Cause."

It was made of fine silk. No small banner, the flag measured one meter by eighty centimeters, its most striking feature being, of course, the brilliant red Rising Sun. Soldiers received lesser quality flags from the government to carry off to war—cotton flags with stitched-on suns. These good luck ensigns gave the young men something to be proud of.

Yoshiharu's flag was special, made of fine silk. It had most likely been purchased by his father, an object of art for an artist.

The signing ceremony took place in the front yard of the Benjiroh House on a hot August day of O Bon. Beyond the murmurs and laughter, cicadae would have buzzed. And men would have wondered as they signed, *What will become of our Yoshiharu?*

"Who were the men who signed?" I ask.

"Oh," says Hideo. "Not just anyone could sign. Not me or the sisters. I was too young. They were girls. My father selected each man carefully. It was an honor to sign the good luck flag. For example, this one says, 'Naval Warrant Officer, Isamu Monma.'"

"Can I meet any of the signers?" I ask.

He answers, "None are left. All dead."

Hideo begins to read the names, pointing to the row of large figures to the right of the globe. "This one, Isao Suzuki, was our next door neighbor," he says. "Next to his sign is Kotaro Ishikawa, the principal where Yoshiharu taught night school. Ginzo Kishi, below the sun—he was a neighboring farmer. His son Toshio is now a leader of our town."

Hideo continues to trace the Kanji marks around the bright globe. "See this one?" he asks. "It's our brother Takataroh who managed the machine shop, Koa Grinder. He signed just below the big slogan that reads, 'Seven Lives Given to Requite One's Debt of Gratitude to Sovereign and Country.' Near Takataroh's sign are the Kato brothers, Kunka and Fugai. Kunka Kato was Yoshiharu's *ikebana* teacher. He gave Yoshiharu his professional name, *kunmei*, meaning bright or crystal. Yoshio Hirokawa, on the left, he was our fire chief, and he wrote, 'Takeyama sub group chief.'"

There they are, fixed in time. Each man had taken up the writing instrument and lovingly inscribed his name— brother, farmer, teacher, neighbor, associate, official—all dead. One element was lacking. There were no young men of Yoshiharu's age. They had preceded him to war.

For a moment in their troubled lives, fifty people of Takeyama rested from their labors. They paused to contemplate the times and say goodbye to one of their own.

Yoshiharu had his banzai. Now it was time to be off to war. He took his fine flag, his bamboo flute, and a small photograph of Masuko. He followed the hundreds of thousands of youths who had gone to war before him. His transport ship left Yokohama by way of Tokyo Bay. It cut south through dangerous waters, prowled by American ships and subs and besieged by enemy aircraft. . .Pacific Ocean. . . Philippine Sea. . .Luzon Strait. . .South China Sea. . .and finally, Luzon Island, Philippines.

Yoshiharu and his shipmates watched expectantly as they skimmed across the South China Sea. They saw the verdant slopes of the Bataan Peninsula glide by. Next they passed the island of Corregidor and beheld, for the first time, one of the world's perfect seaports—Manila Bay. Only the rusty skeletons of sunken American ships marred the calm waters of the bay. The troop transport arrived safely in Manila Harbor, fifteen hundred miles from the homeland of Japan.

Each soldier was issued field equipment: standard steel helmet; aluminum water bottle with shoulder strap; mess kit and other essentials including covered basket for holding a day's ration of rice; haversack; half-tent (also served as rain cape); entrenching tool; ammunition belt; and the *Arisaka* 6.5mm type 38 rifle with bayonet. Field clothing included: tropical field cap with neck guard; khaki tunic and breeches; knee-length shorts; standard ankle boots or split-toed tabi made of rubber feet and canvas uppers; and puttees (leggings wrapped around lower legs for protection).

Fully equipped, Yoshiharu was transferred to the Bataan Peninsula with his outfit, ready to meet the enemy.

He waited on Bataan.

Bataan, 1945
(Boisclaire collection)

Regulation issue flag, gun, and canteen *(Boisclaire; artifacts courtesy of Mo Lovely, collector of WWII memorabilia)*

Chapter 7

Bataan

The Bataan Peninsula juts into the South China Sea to form the western shore of Manila Bay. After the fall of Manila, in December 1941, the jungle-covered appendage provided American troops with a solid defensive position. A few scattered plantations and small towns—Mariveles, Cabcaben, Lamao, Orion, Pilar, Orani—dotted the habitable areas. One main road crossed Bataan between the towns of Bagac and Pilar. Another skirted the perimeter. The rest of the terrain choked with thick forests of vines, hardwoods and undergrowth; rugged mountains; impassable marshes and bogs; and quagmires. All these rendered

Bataan nearly impenetrable.

The jagged tip of Bataan plunges into the sea, project-ing a narrow finger of land. It points to Corregidor, three miles out, an island fortress guarding the bay—what had been General Douglas MacArthur's headquarters for a short time in 1942.

From the tip of Bataan, the coast returns north, creat-ing a barrier between Mariveles Bay and the South China Sea. From there the land forms an arc of beach. Mariveles nestles at the apex of the bay. The coast sweeps past villages, jungle, tidal streams, swamps, deltas, sandy and rocky stretches, seawalls and piers before reaching Manila—meandering east, north, east again, and finally south, in an irregular pocket, to form the huge body of tranquil water called Manila Bay. Bataan faces Manila to the east, thirty miles distant.

Amidst this setting Filipino and American allies waged war against Japanese troops in a bitter four-month siege in 1942. The Japanese squeezed the defenders onto the peninsula, cutting them off from the world. Allied soldiers contracted jungle diseases and ran out of food and sup-plies. No reinforcements or lifesaving provisions came to relieve them. No ships appeared to evacuate the belea-guered Americans.

Casualties mounted on both sides as Japanese forces pushed south—Pilar-Bagac, Orion, Mount Samat, Limay. MacArthur was ordered out and withdrew to Australia, leaving his men to defend Bataan as best they could with inadequate weaponry. Weak from starvation, outnumbered ten to one, they fell before the massive Japanese offen-sive. Surrender took place at the village of Lamao on April 9, 1942. Since that day, Bataan remained as ever, draped with inhospitable jungle, laced with danger and blight.

When Yoshiharu arrived in 1944, Bataan provided a defense for the Japanese occupation troops. Wreckage littered the jungle floor—blown-up artillery, spent shells, ruined trucks—all reminders that a bitter war had been fought on Bataan. The ravages left by warfare healed slowly. Trees grew up where bombs and fires had denuded the jungle. Thick vines and grass crept over the scarred soil. Jungle sounds resounded anew.

Japanese soldiers now took positions within and around the small villages scattered along the coastal road. Yoshiharu's unit would have been based somewhere on the primitive peninsula, presumably between Mariveles and Orani.

By this time the war taxed Japan heavily. Supplies had dwindled at home and in the outermost reaches of the new Japanese empire, including Bataan. Food, medicine, and ammunition were hard to obtain. Just a small daily ration of rice was all that could be counted on, in addition to whatever could be haggled from villagers.

If the jungle seemed unfriendly, the villagers proved to be more so. Many had fled from their Japanese over-lords, deserting their gardens and homes. Those still living on Bataan were uncooperative, at best.

We can only guess what happened there. Without doubt, Yoshiharu and his stalwart companions did their best in this hostile land. Despite the hardships, they would not have failed to notice the novel sights around them.

Stranded far from home, the young men would have marveled at the ever-changing face of the bay. On a clear day they might patrol inland to climb a peak for an even better look. Mount Samat, Mount Limay, or any number of unnamed ridges afforded beautiful bird's-eye vistas. The soldiers could overlook the sea lanes, counting Japanese ships as they bypassed Bataan on their way to and from Manila. Or they could watch Mitsubishi airplanes roar overhead maintaining surveillance of the land and sea.

A lonely land was this place called Bataan. Most likely rumors spread, terrible rumors of bombings in the homeland, lost battles, changing tides of war. Was Japan losing? Were the soldiers' families still alive? Young hearts ached, like thousands of others did at remote posts all over Asia. They ached to know the truth, but how could they? No letters came from home, and their commanders discounted all rumors as lies. Dread descended upon the guardians of Bataan, who in reality became its prisoners more than keepers. Loneliness and doom settled in as thick and heavy as the humid air.

Each evening, eerie shadows fell across the jungle camp. It was then the unseasoned soldiers would hear the haunting song of Yoshiharu's flute as it echoed through the trees and quieted their fears.

Young men would have gathered and talked, in hushed tones, of home. They would have started small cookfires. While waiting for their rice to cook, they would have brought out their cherished flags and read familiar names and glorious promises.

Having retired their flags and eaten their rice, the youths would have braced themselves for hordes of malaria-bearing mosquitos. Then came the nighttime downpour that made tropical camping miserable.

Despite the unfriendly jungle, Yoshiharu's flag remained safe and dry—he made sure of it. When he took the flag out of his pack he would have wondered if he would ever carry it down the narrow road between the tall bamboo that led to the Benjiroh House.

A constant thread of love tied Yoshiharu to his home. How he longed to return. As he waited, he would have remembered each member of his family: the little sisters, the brothers, and his father, Shigeji. He would have thought of Masuko, fifteen hundred miles away, as he gazed at her captivating image on the tiny snapshot. He would have prayed to be reunited someday.

As he waited, he would have thought all these thoughts and more. . .

That was until the Americans returned.

Chapter 8

Death, Life, and the Flag

"O Death, where is your sting?
O Hades where is your victory?"

1 Corinthians 15:55

No one knew of Yoshiharu's death. Few Japanese surrendered on Bataan. Life went on in Yokosuka, and soon the war ended. Shohzoh returned home; Yoshiharu did not.

"For three years we waited," says Hideo sadly. "We never heard from Yoshiharu. Maybe he sent letters, but we didn't receive any. Then came the telegram that shattered all hope. It arrived March 18, 1948. According to the Army, Yoshiharu died at Mount Samat on February 15, 1945. We held a funeral. After awhile Masuko disappeared and was reported to have died of a broken heart."

The events of the next era tumble out. Takataroh remained in Tokyo. The sisters married. The second son, Shohzoh, married into another family and moved away. After a time Shigeji died. Hideo inherited the Benjiroh House. He did not farm the land. Instead, he worked at the U.S. naval base in Yokosuka.

Although the Army had declared Yoshiharu dead and funeral rites had been performed, the family still found it difficult to accept the death of their beloved Yoshiharu. They hoped beyond hope that he had married and started a new life in the Philippine Islands, ashamed to come home.

I can visualize Hideo on his return to the Benjiroh House night after night. He would remember Yoshiharu, fifteen hundred miles away, and he would long to tell him, "Yoshiharu, it's all right to come home."

Hideo retired in 1992. The year before, he traveled to Bataan to see the place where Yoshiharu had waited and died in the lonely jungle so many years before. Hideo wanted to find a remembrance of his lost brother. He harbored the secret hope of meeting Yoshiharu there.

He constructed a small memorial on Mount Samat and brought home a container of soil taken from the slopes.

Just as the gloomy facts are settling in, Hideo brings out a map and points to Mount Samat on the Bataan Peninsula, Island of Luzon. We spot Mariveles, the bay where the Americans landed and Japanese soldiers fought to the death.

We trace along the coast from Mariveles to Cabcaben,

where Jesse Campbell, the American, found the flag. I tell Campbell's story—the story of a small patrol, a banana plantation, a sniper, a dead Japanese soldier, and two flags.

For Jesse Campbell, the war had a better ending. He plucked Yoshiharu's treasured ensign from the death, killing, and agony that engulfed Bataan. He returned home. He folded the Rising Sun, tucked it in an envelope, and stashed it away.

Now, after fifty-one years, the flag has come home to rest. Yes, Yoshiharu died fifty years ago; Hideo knows it. It is O Bon night, 1995, and once again, Hideo will grieve for his lost brother.

Tracing map of Bataan Peninsula *(Shishido)*

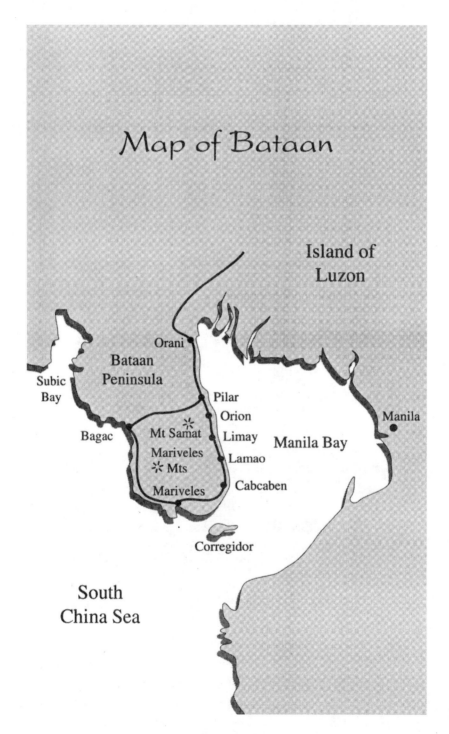

Chapter 9

The Mystery

"Be yourself first, then go to your own funeral and let God forever after be All in All."

Oswald Chambers

Our second day with the Tsunoi family is reserved for newspaper interviews. We return and enter the presence of the dark house backed up against the curtain of bamboo. It hugs the shadows and seems to be sulking, as if waiting for someone or something.

The vacant house breathes not a word of the large family that toiled and lived harmoniously from 1886 to 1989. Yoshiharu would have lived out his life in this house.

We gather in the new house built by Hideo. Five reporters present themselves. Among them we meet Kumi Ushida of the Sankai Press and Aoki Susumu of the Kanagawa Shinbun.

With the uncertainties of the first day behind, Hideo seems more relaxed and outgoing. Atsuko's extrovertive personality also shines through.

Hideo and I retell our stories and pose for photographs. The reporters take notes and look through Yoshiharu's things. In due time the polite reporters leave. Larry and I also prepare to say goodbye to our new friends, Hideo and Atsuko. Before we do, I make a startling discovery.

Yoshiharu's mementos have been spread out on the tatami floor. The reporters have seen them. I walk over for a final look. It seems there are twice as many photographs as I saw yesterday. Perhaps Hideo brought them out for the first time in many years while he spent a lonely night of remembrance for his brother.

Recorded on film, I see Yoshiharu's face, a serious looking young man, fixed forever in activities of life: a flower show with students, dressed in his black robe, now a western suit, and finally, a somber, uniformed Yoshiharu. It is a set of tiny twin photographs that catches my eye. I hold one up and ask, "Can I have this? There are two."

Hideo answers, "O.K."

We leave the jungle, the bugs, and the sulking old house. Hideo and Atsuko take us to lunch, then house us in a fine Japanese style hotel on Miura-Kaigan beach.

In the seclusion of our room Larry and I stretch out on futons. I flip open my wallet to study the small photograph now in my possession, but I stare past it, deep in thought.

Larry asks, "Are you O.K.? You seem sad."

"Just thinking," I say. "I'll miss having the flag. But look at this. It could be just as important. I think Yoshiharu was a Christian. His family didn't know it."

I hand the photo to Larry, who looks at me, smiling, and says, "How did you get this?"

I reply, "I asked Hideo if I could have it. There were two, and he said, 'O.K.' A fair trade, don't you think? I traded it for the flag."

The mysterious photo measures a mere one and one half by two inches. It shows Yoshiharu's framed portrait under the cross of Jesus. We wonder what it means.

The first person to see our new possession is Kumi the reporter. She arrives in the morning to take us on tour of the U.S. Naval Base at Yokosuka. Here we encounter, by chance, another reporter from yesterday—Aoki Susumu.

Aoki, Yvonne, and Larry
aboard USS *Independence*
(Ushida)

Kumi and Yvonne at U.S.
naval base
(Boisclaire)

Later, at lunch, I bring out the small photograph for Kumi's inspection. At this time we discover three rows of Kanji penciled on the back of Yoshiharu's photo.

Kumi reads two lines, "'Tsunoi, Yoshiharu. 1938, July 7, born.' His birthday," she announces.

"No," I counter, "He was born in 1914. This would be his born again day as a Christian."

 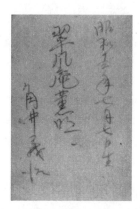

Kumi gasps in surprise. But we have no time to discuss Yoshiharu's possible religion. Kumi takes us to the train station where we hear a string of places we could go: "Moriyama, Kusatsu, Kyoto, Takatsuki, Settsu, Osaka." We choose the Shinkansen Osaka, a bullet train headed west.

We leave Yokosuka and set out to sample the beauty, culture, and people of Japan. Our first stop is Takatsuki, near Osaka, at a Christian base called Youth With A Mission. The YWAM folks welcome us and brief us on Japan. Three days later we wend our way to the island of Shikoku.

Armed with a few Japanese phrases, we ride trains past beautiful beaches and pockets of farm land tucked between steep mountains, green hills, and conspicuous industrial sites. We sleep on gravelly pillows and firm futons. We eat rice and sushi with chopsticks. We bow and use the curious squat toilets and learn to take a proper bath. We encounter the honest, polite, and abundantly helpful citizens of Japan.

The little photograph travels with us on bullet train,

slow train, bus, car, everywhere. So too, my favorite illustrated newspaper article by Aoki Susumu: Hideo and Yvonne with the flag.

The media paves the way. We have hit the press in two national and three local newspapers. It works like magic: show the article and see eyes widen. People look from me to the press clipping and back to me, then say, "You?" I tap my nose in the Japanese way, indicating me.

Next, they read the lines. Then comes the drama as people clutch their hearts and say, *"Arigato gozaimasu,"* meaning thank you. Some show their gratitude with tears, others with handshakes. It happens time and again.

Finally, we announce, "Mystery," to the interested seat companion and show Yoshiharu's photograph. We ask if the man pictured could be a Christian.

"Ah, yes," they say, "But very difficult to be a Christian during the war."

And so we move across Japan. Soon we arrive at the beautiful coastal area of Tosashimizu and meet Michio Takenaka, an electrical engineer who also serves as a Christian pastor. He holds up Yoshiharu's picture. Talking through an interpreter, he says, "See this little picture of yours? Had Yoshiharu carried it to war and his officer found it, what do you think would have happened?"

We do not know.

"The officer would have beheaded Yoshiharu on the spot," replies Michio. "Thus the snapshot was left at home."

Michio goes on. "Yoshiharu's government prohibited Christianity. Your western religion represented the God of the enemy. Military leaders declared Shintoism the state religion and required the citizenry to worship at Shinto shrines. Those who embraced the God of the West were considered traitors. Many Christians were imprisoned. Most died in chains."

What was a Christian to do? Professing faith brought dishonor to the family name, separation, and imprisonment. Yoshiharu, respected artist; disowned, disinherited, banished? Son of Shigeji, community leader; disgracing his family that way? Imprisonment, death, war—hard choices for a son. And Yoshiharu loved his family so.

Yoshiharu made a choice. He could have declared his forbidden faith and gone to prison with other Christians. Instead, he went quietly to war, knowing he faced death. But for a Christian, death holds the final victory. At all costs Yoshiharu avoided bringing disgrace upon his family. He would not mar the Tsunoi name nor send his father's gray head to the grave in sorrow and shame.

We learn all this but still cannot crack the code on the back of Yoshiharu's photo. The first row (right side) reads Yoshiharu Tsunoi. The last row (left) stands for the born again date. The middle characters have not been deciphered by anyone thus far; not until we meet the professor, Takao Takahashi.

We meet the Takahashi family at Oyabu Onsen, a one-hundred-year-old hot springs resort popular with Japanese families. Takao Takahashi is a philosophy professor at Kumamoto University in Kyushu, Japan. He has studied at Oxford. The Japanese professor finds the miniature photograph fascinating. He ponders its mystery for an entire day before rendering his analysis.

"The photo is a metaphor and full of symbolism," Takao explains. "This was prepared by a very intelligent man with a purpose in mind. It's a funeral. The man Yoshiharu drew his own funeral portrait, framed it, then set up a shrine. People only made such displays for funerals. It represented death of the old Yoshiharu."

Takao goes on to read the middle row on the back of Yoshiharu's photograph: "Each Kanji word can have more than one meaning. It can be interpreted different ways. This first character, *sui*, is green or cool. Next we see *ran*, meaning storm or fresh air of the mountain. Together, we have *suiran*. This means green air of the mountain. The third word stands for small cottage or secret room, like a tea ceremony house. The fourth is smell or feel. This last one I can't read."

Using *ikebana* to express his Christian faith, Yoshiharu proclaimed death to his old self and a new life in Jesus. He photographed the display and hid two small pictures, providing his family with a posthumous witness of his faith.

After our departure with the Takahashi family we return to the YWAM base. Intrigued by the photograph, David Hamilton of YWAM enlarges it by means of a computer scanner. The blow-up reveals more of Yoshiharu's mystery. The scroll appears to be hand drawn. Traces of Kanji are inscribed along the cross. The flowers are gladioli, with three sprays reaching upward. Yoshiharu placed his portrait in a low position under Jesus. The Christ looks over him, as if to protect and guide. A placard is placed beside the portrait. On it the character *suiran* appears again and the Kanji symbol for flower.

Later I would read a book explaining *ikebana*. Japanese people consider themselves to be intimate with nature. *Ikebana* creates unity between man and the natural world. Flowers set the mood—each one symbolizes an emotion. Yoshiharu arranged his gladioli sprays in three levels. In *ikebana* the levels represent, from top to bottom, heaven, man, and earth. To Christians, the three divisions signify Trinity: Father, Son, and Holy Ghost. The gladiola represents secret.

So this was Yoshiharu's secret. He kept it well hidden. Not even his family knew.

At Oyabu Onsen with Japanese owner *(Boisclaire)*

Larry Boisclaire at Oyabu Onsen *(Boisclaire)*

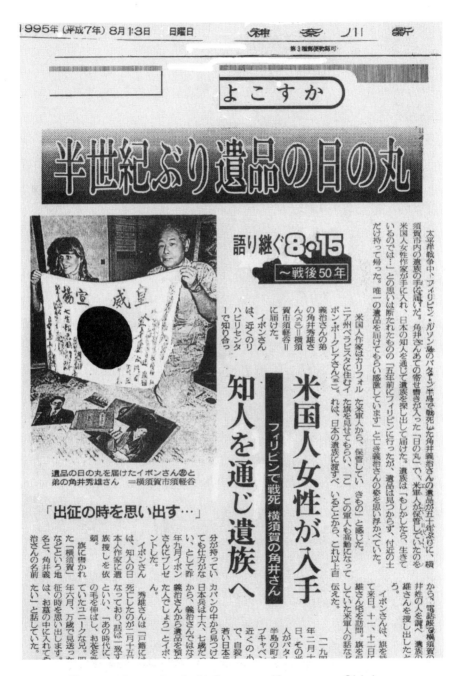

Press release by Aoki Susumu, Kanagawa Shinbun,
August 13, 1995

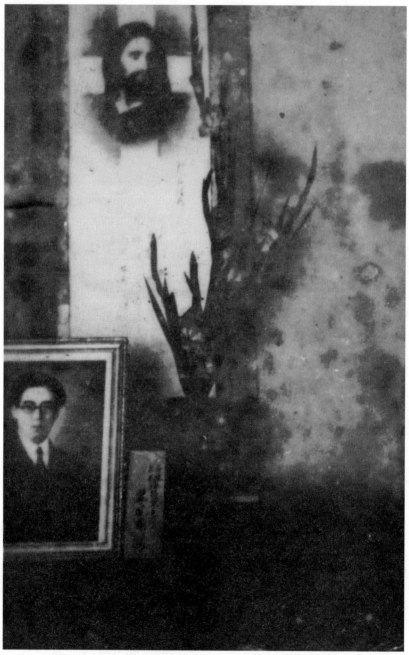

Enlargement of Yoshiharu's secret photograph
(Produced by YWAM)

Chapter 10

Tapestry of God

By this time, we cannot help but be amazed at the chain of events that has linked us with the flag.

For a full half-century, from 1945 on, Jesse Campbell held the flag. So how would I, Yvonne, happen to meet Jesse?

I became a nurse, an unlikely mid-life change for this mother of two, self-employed draftsperson, and outdoor-loving housewife who did not give a thought to hospitals or sickness or doctors' offices. But foreign missions appealed to my husband and me. For that reason, nursing seemed to be a valuable skill to acquire. Besides, our children were grown, and attending college would be no problem for me.

I completed nursing school, then took a position at Redding Medical Center. After working a few years, an opening in Cardiac Rehab came along—a teaching position highly desired by registered nurses. I applied and was delighted to get the job.

So where was Jesse? Time pursued him and caught him with a heart attack. He enrolled in Cardiac Rehab. There he met the petite blond nurse named Yvonne.

I first saw the flag in August 1994 during Japan's week of O Bon, fifty years after Yoshiharu took it to war. Jesse Campbell felt a tug on his heart. He retrieved that old war flag from hiding and placed it in my hands. He could have saved the flag for his heirs or donated it to a museum. Or he could have fetched a good price through an agent specializing in Japanese war memorabilia.

Suddenly the flag was mine, and its writings told a story. I had no clues as to the meaning, neither did the few Japanese-speaking people I knew. The writing was an old style of Kanji.

A co-worker, Martha Mitchell, put me in contact with Andrew Gebert the interpreter. I sent him an enlarged photograph of the flag, then waited through the winter of 1994.

The year rolled into 1995. The phone rang on a rainy February day. A New York accent asked for Yvonne. It was Andrew, and he told me the banner had belonged to Yoshiharu Tsunoi of Takeyama. He asked, "What will you do with the flag?"

My sister, husband, and I had already talked and agreed—if surviving family were found, the flag should be returned to Japan. Our decision pleased Andrew, and he sought assistance from across the ocean.

In Tokyo, Andrew's friend Shinichi Nishimura took appropriate action. He began calling everyone in the Kanagawa prefecture with the name of Tsunoi. His eighth try struck gold. He had on the line Hideo Tsunoi, who said, "Yes, my brother Yoshiharu Tsunoi died in the Philippines during the war."

The news reached us in April. "What will you do?" asked Andrew.

"We will go to Japan and return the flag in person," I replied.

Dates and vacations must be arranged and tickets purchased. Soon, anticipation turned into reality. We had obstacles to overcome: the dollar was down, the yen up, a crazy fanatic cult lurked the subways of Japan with poison gas and as always, earthquakes threatened Japan. American-Japanese tensions mounted as the fiftieth anniversary of VJ Day neared. Our trip looked costly and complex. Where would we go, what would we do, two English-limited Anglos traveling in Japan?

We could mail the flag. Better yet, had not Tsunoi offered to travel to The States himself? We considered our options and examined our motives. We were hoping to reach across political and national boundaries to touch a family person-to-person. Would Jesse and other veterans consider this a betrayal? It was not intended as such. Something inside compelled us to go forward with our plans.

We picked August to coincide with Andrew's presence in Japan. He would be conducting business then. Andrew warned us—August travel is very demanding in Japan. This part of summer drips with humidity and heat. Families hop the trains and head to the beaches or mountain resorts. It is O Bon, the time of vacation for all of Japan.

As the time approached, we considered canceling the trip. We prayed for guidance. Our God has His own way of answering prayer. He rarely tells us directly what to do.

Instead, He opens or closes doors.

A door opened through the Christians at YWAM. On the day we made contact, the friendly YWAM host, Joseph Celona, said, "Do come, please. You can stay as long as you wish."

Presently, the day of departure arrived. We boarded the Boeing and set out from San Francisco. Hours later we set foot on Rising Sun domain.

As we look back on these events the past falls into place. Beyond mere circumstance, beyond coincidence, these events were directed by a master's hand. God had woven together people, places, and events to form the complex tapestry that brought us to Japan.

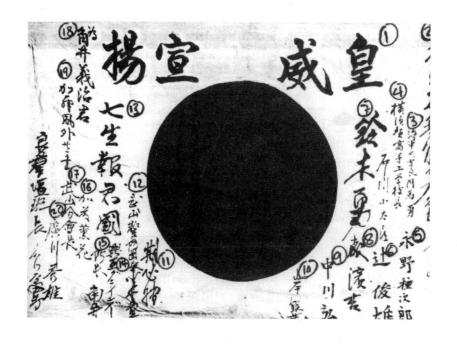

Numerical coding of flag by Andrew Gebert.
Letter on following page.

Dear Yvonne,

Sorry it has taken me so long to get back to you. I have been busy with a number of other projects. I also had to enlist the help of a Japanese friend to decipher the more stylized writing. These inscriptions were no doubt made at a sending-off for Kadoi (Tsunoi is an alternate pronunciation) Yoshiharu. Thus, it is signed by his school principal (4), his boss (15), and friends.

As far as locating any surviving relations, an ad in a local paper that includes Yokosuka (Kanagawa Prefecture) would be the best bet. Also 16 and 19 are pen names of some sort, possibly painters or artists, and that could be a clue. If there are any surviving relations, the return of the flag would no doubt be deeply appreciated and I would help in whatever way I can. Again, apologies for the delay.

1   Promote and Advance the Imperial Prestige
2   Yoshiharu—Live for the Grand and Eternal Cause!
3   Naval Warrant Officer, Monma Isamu
4   Yokosuka Industrial High School Principal,
        Ishikawa Kotaro
5   Nagano Tanejiro
6   Tsuji Toshio
7   Suzuki Isao
8   Sai(?) Hamakichi
9   Nakagawa Hiroshi
10 Kishi Ginzo
11 With the Determination for Certain Victory
12 Takeyama (Civil) Defense Unit Chief, Yamamoto
13 Seven Lives, Given to Requite (One's Debt of
        Gratitude to) Sovereign and Country
14 Koa Grinder
15 Manager, Manamii
16 Kato Kunka
17 Takeyama sub Group chief
18 For Kadoi (Tsunio) Yoshiharu
19 Kato Fugai
20 Hirokawa Yoshio

Best regards and good luck,

Andrew Gebert

Left to right, Nishimura, Tsunoi, Gebert
(Shishido)

Chapter 11

Though Dead, He Speaks

By faith Abel offered to God
    A more excellent sacrifice than Cain,
Through which he obtained witness
    That he was righteous,
God testifying of his gifts;
    And through it he being dead still speaks.

Hebrews 11:4

We return to the Tsunoi home for our last day in Japan, our objective being to inform Hideo and Atsuko of Yoshiharu's secret religion. The decision to do so has not been made lightly. The last thing we want is to bring more grief to this already heartbroken family. Seeking advice, we are assured the family would want to know, just as Yoshiharu intended.

We know the truth and they do not. . .by faith Yoshiharu went to war. . .by faith he believed his message would be delivered someday. If he did not want it so, then why were the photographs left behind?

We arrive by train in Yokosuka. Hideo and Atsuko meet us at the station. They received us cordially two weeks earlier. This time, they greet us with open arms, and we return to the two houses enclosed in their sanctuary of trees.

We are surprised and delighted to meet Tatsuko, Yoshiharu's beloved youngest sister, the one to whom he was closest. We learn that Yoshiharu has three surviving siblings. Besides Hideo and Tatsuko, another sister, Kiku, remains alive and well in Tokyo.

Tatsuko speaks no English. Through Hideo's interpretation, we chat amiably. Tatsuko answers my final questions to fill out the rich life of Yoshiharu Tsunoi. The surviving siblings still adore their older brother, fifty-one years later. By 1995 he seems like a saint.

Hideo brings out an album. He has arranged all of Yoshiharu's photographs in there. I turn the pages looking for the twin to the picture I carry. I find it on the third page—a small photograph of Yoshiharu under the cross of Jesus. Slipping it from the pocket, I turn it over just to see. It has no writing on the backside. Only ours carries the message—the message we must now deliver.

I bring out my copy. We ask Hideo to read the back. "1938, July 7, born," he says.

"What does it mean?" we ask.

"Probably, Yoshiharu received his *ikebana* name that time," answers Hideo.

"Yes," says Larry, "but there's another interpretation. Born as a Christian in 1938."

Hideo, Atsuko, and Tatsuko exchange surprised looks. The women begin conversing in earnest. They whisper words we cannot understand. Then the sisters-in-law embrace, and tears fill their eyes.

The three realize why we are here. Their brother has left a message. Yoshiharu did not know it would require fifty years, nor did he know it would be delivered by Americans. He never came home. Instead his flag did, fifty years overdue. His secret message follows close behind.

The moment Yoshiharu trusted in is here. We, his Christian brother and sister, come face to face with his earthly brother and sister, and Larry relays the news. "When we brought you the flag you expressed how thrilled you were to receive it, but how sad this was for you. Your hopes were dashed by the final reality of Yoshiharu's death. But now we can tell you that your brother lives. The Christian Bible teaches us that Christians never die. That means Yoshiharu now dwells with Jesus in heaven."

Tatsuko's face glows. She says, "Yes, it is so. I didn't know then, but I know now. My brother was a Christian."

Then we add, "A great chasm separates man from God. Yet God welcomes all men to trust Him. Yoshiharu trusted in Jesus and bridged that huge gap to eternity. As fellow Christians, we believe we will see Yoshiharu someday."

This completes our journey. We set out on a mission of good will, not quite sure of why or if we should go. We finished by giving a message of hope, a gift to his family from a deceased brother. How would they receive his gift?

By faith we traveled to Japan for our appointed time with Hideo. We do not know what would have occurred

had we resisted the prompting to journey here. This we
know: Yoshiharu, though dead, still speaks.

Yoshiharu Tsunoi,
self portrait
(Courtesy of Tsunoi)

Chapter 12

The Closure

The time has come for Larry and me to return to America. Hideo and Atsuko have brought us to the airport, and we bid our sad farewells. Larry and I board a Boeing 747. She lifts quickly from the runway, swings over the coast of Japan, and heads across the Pacific Ocean.

Larry's fingers encircle mine as we share a silent prayer of thanksgiving. I look back and catch a glimpse of Mount Fuji, towering above the valleys and peaks of Japan, framed by the afterglow of the setting sun. Wonder fills my mind as I recall the rich blessings that have flowed from this faraway land, the Land of the Rising Sun. I think of the gracious YWAM people: Joseph, Andy, James, Esther, David, Sika, and the other friends we have made: Hideo, Atsuko, Kumi, Aoki, Takao, Michio, Kiyo, Shin, Andrew. I think of the people we learned of but will never meet: Masuko, Shigeji, Hisa, and all those who signed the flag.

Mostly though, I think of Yoshiharu. A great chasm exists between Yoshiharu and me. Nationality, generations, and wars cast our lives in separate spheres.

We continue to climb, thousands of feet above the Pacific Ocean by now. Darkness rapidly overtakes us as we flee from the setting sun. Again, except for the crew and a few passengers, Larry and I are the only Caucasians on board. Concealed from the pilot, the crew, and the passengers nestled around us, I carry a small photo of Yoshiharu Tsunoi. Both to and from Japan, we harbored an object of great value to the long-dead Christian soldier.

We soar over the water below. In silent meditation I rejoice in all that has been revealed. Yet, I can't help but continue the search for answers.

I consider what might have happened to Yoshiharu on Bataan. We have no diary to reveal the facts. Given the circumstances of the war, however, I imagine the weary days preceding that fateful February 15. We left Yoshiharu waiting on the jungle-covered peninsula of Bataan. . .

Yoshiharu Tsunoi the soldier
(Courtesy of Tsunoi)

Jungle obscured the face of Bataan, concealing a small Japanese camp. Soldiers of this outfit had full assignments, though some languished in camp, sick with malaria or any number of jungle diseases. The fit and able-bodied maintained vehicles, equipment, and guns, besides receiving and relaying important messages from headquarters. There were sanitation, food, water, and ordnance to attend to, in addition to scouting for the enemy. Food stores dwindled. The soldiers prowled villages and small plantations searching for foodstuffs. Some men hauled clean water from local artesian wells. Others went on patrol.

The steaming jungle was wet and hostile, choked by vines and haunted by vipers and leeches and unknown ills. When Yoshiharu ventured from camp, he donned his heavy protective gear: tunic, breeches, tabi, puttees. Next, he hoisted his haversack, canteen, and rifle. His flute, flag, and the snapshot of Masuko would be safely stashed in a pocket or pack.

Yoshiharu patrolled the camp perimeter and found nothing but forests, vines, impassable marshes and swamps, and quagmires. He might patrol inland to watch Manila Bay from the peak of Mount Samat, stopping to inspect any war wreckage he stumbled upon. Having achieved his purpose, he might remove his pack and heavy clothing and bathe in the cool waters of the Belolo River.

Yoshiharu sweltered by day and swatted mosquitos by night. He saw vines grow and smelled mold as it crept into his pack to spoil his food, rot his clothes, and ruin his gun. He heard the click, buzz, hum of the jungle. Yet, in these harsh environs, he noted each beautiful flower growing wild in the bush.

Yoshiharu endured the long winter of 1944. The New Year came and went. He thought of home and still waited. Early each morning, he arose to see the sun rise over Manila and turn the bay pink. Its newborn glory danced on the bay in a kaleidoscope of unpredictable color—pink, gold,

silver, blue, gray. He studied the skyline to the southwest
and saw jungle rising sharply to hills, then ridges, climax-
ing at Mount Bataan, forty-seven hundred feet up. He
watched dark rain clouds roll up the Mariveles Mountains,
then dump their watery loads in tropical torrents. January
passed him by. He was still waiting in camp when the
breathless scout arrived with an urgent report. The Americans were coming on that dripping hot February day.

They came like a flock of homing pigeons returning
after a long flight—Jesse Campbell and a battalion of other
fresh young men from The States.

Jesse had left his hometown months before. At age
twenty-one, he said his goodbyes in California and joined
the Indiana National Guard. After basic training he was
shipped to the South Pacific as a member of the 38th Division of the U.S. Army. Jesse's ship joined the huge armada
that reclaimed the Philippines. They traveled to Leyte Island where General Douglas MacArthur struck his feet on
Philippine shores, and the troops he commanded engaged
the enemy.

Campbell's ship traveled north through island-
studded waters until it reached Luzon. The ship anchored
in Subic Bay. There, the forces split. The 152nd and 149th
infantry of the 38th Division went ashore to rout the large
enemy emplacement dug in at Zig Zag Pass. Campbell's
outfit, the 151st infantry, backtracked south by sea, skirt-
ing the peninsula of Bataan. Their objective: secure
Corregidor and other parts south.

They came from Subic Bay, bypassing the jungle
and swamps and rugged mountains of Bataan. They round-
ed the southernmost finger of Bataan and headed into
the mouth of Mariveles Bay.

The Americans disembarked on the morning of February 15, 1945 and were opposed only by a brief round of
machine gun and rifle fire. By this time, many Japanese
soldiers had died of other causes. Bataan, that strategic

defensive stronghold, took its toll of Japanese in 1945, just as it had done to Americans in 1942. Starvation and disease had decimated the troops.

During that first night, seventy-five to one hundred Japanese soldiers attacked the American perimeter three miles northeast of Mariveles. The aftermath of fighting left sixty Japanese soldiers and a few Americans dead.

Japanese guerrillas on Bataan reacted to the invasion by quickly destroying crossings over the many tidal streams along the coastal route.

Meanwhile, in a pincher maneuver, the U.S. Army's 1st infantry, East Force, moved south from Orani along the coast road of Bataan. They encountered no Japanese resistance, just irritating delays caused by destroyed bridges.

The Americans reached Orion on February 15. That night, three hundred Japanese soldiers attacked the 1st infantry. Close fighting ensued, leaving eighty of the weakened Japanese dead to eleven Americans. This, and the simultaneous night attack at Mariveles, marked the end of organized Japanese resistance on the peninsula. Survivors scattered into the jungle or fled toward the peaks of Bataan. The war was over for the exhausted Japanese occupation forces.

On February 16, patrols of the 151st infantry combed the Mariveles area for enemy troops. The bulk of the Americans boarded landing craft and headed to Corregidor with the assignment of retaking the captured American fortress.

On February 17, Jesse Campbell's antitank outfit moved east from Mariveles parallel to the shoreline of Bataan. No enemy tanks came out to oppose them. No Japanese were encountered at all as the men inched along Manila Bay to rendezvous with the 1st infantry.

When Campbell reached the village of Cabcaben, a group of Filipinos hailed his group and made this request:

"Could you take us to our banana plantation? It's been occupied by Japanese soldiers since 1942."

Jesse, his best friend, and two or three others agreed to go. Led by the Filipinos, they entered the vines and bamboo stands, walking approximately one mile to reach the plantation.

They were almost there when stopped in their tracks by gunfire. A shot rang out, then several more came their way. Ever so cautiously, Jesse's patrol approached the hut. Inside they found a soldier, very young but dead.

It was not possible to tell if the youth had been killed by the shots just fired. He may have died in the honorable Japanese way, having saved the last bullet for himself.

The dead soldier carried a flag on his body. Jesse's friend took it. Another flag lay folded in a pack on the floor. Jesse Campbell picked it up. It was February 18, 1945.

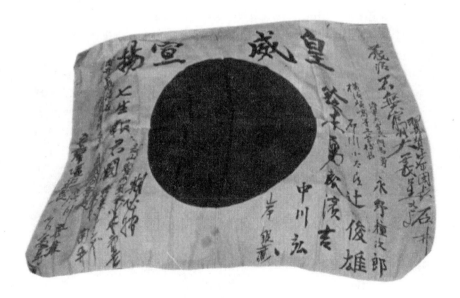

(Shishido)

The dull drone of the Boeing's engines is all I hear except for the occasional cough or stirring of a passenger. Opening my window shade, I can see no farther than the flashing lights. It's a dark, moonless night. I wonder what keeps this huge ship airborne.

I also find myself wondering how Yoshiharu's flag arrived at the plantation near Cabcaben. The Army notice received by his father stated that Yoshiharu died at Mount Samat on February 15, 1945, ten miles away through swampy jungle or twenty miles by road.

My mind returns to Cabcaben where Jesse Campbell and Yoshiharu Tsunoi presumably met.

I try to picture what happened on that last day. I can only speculate.

Cabcaben, circa 1940
(Boisclaire collection)

Yoshiharu could have waited in the cabana to meet death on February 18. Although thirty-one years old, his small stature and Oriental agelessness resulted in a youthful appearance. It could have been his body. According to Hideo, however, Yoshiharu would have found it impossible to fire at another human being. From what I know of Yoshiharu, I believe it. Another factor clouds the issue: the dead young soldier had two flags. Yoshiharu had only one.

More likely, I believe, Yoshiharu laid down his life and flag between Orion and Mount Samat three days earlier. . .

Let us assume that Yoshiharu's concern for others did not cease when he went to war. In his kindly way, he could have befriended a younger soldier. They could have made a pact. Whoever survived the war would carry the precious flags back home.

So it was, the frantic but inevitable day arrived, the day of February 15. Suppose it arrived to find Yoshiharu's outfit hastily destroying bridges and trapped in the pincher movement. That night they became embroiled in the last organized battle between American and Japanese troops— the battle at Orion.

What would Yoshiharu's last prayer have been—for his family; for deliverance? In spite of his prayers, he died. Never again would he see the rising sun over Manila, nor gaze in wonder at the huge pocket of shimmering water safely sheltering Manila Harbor. Nor would he walk victorious down the narrow road that led to the Benjiro House.

The trusted youthful companion could have fled from the death zone with the treasured flags, both his and Yoshiharu's. He could have fought his way through the thick jungle, frightened and alone, to reach Cabcaben. He could have burst through the cabin door exhausted, out of breath, and weeping in his heart at the loss of his friend, perhaps returning to the very cabana where he and Yoshiharu had stayed before the last day.

The boy made his final stand two days later. He relinquished two flags in a cabana, at a banana plantation just outside Cabcaben, while Yoshiharu's lifeless body remained at Mount Samat.

Filipino cabana, 1945
(Boisclaire collection)

Forty-six years passed before the younger brother, Hideo, walked the same Philippine soil where Yoshiharu met his premature death. Four more years passed before the flag returned, full circle, to the village of Takeyama where the old house still lingers under the shadow of bamboo.

Yoshiharu has left us with another unsolved mystery, along with many unanswered questions. The Boeing trav-

els swiftly on the jet stream. Questions pursue, allowing
no rest for my weary mind. I search for answers.

   His faith. How did a citizen of Japan become a Christian in 1938? Yoshiharu's suit hints of a Western influence.
He often traveled to flower shows. Could he have met a
missionary?

   What of the shrine and scroll? The scroll looks as if
Yoshiharu drew it himself, along with his own portrait. He
would have hidden these in a secret place, upstairs or away
from home.

   The scroll has never been found. The Kanji characters written along the cross do not help. They are too faint
to be deciphered. What explanations might this writing
disclose?

   His flag. What of the patriarchs who signed the flag?
What secrets passed to eternity with them?

   Isamu Monma, the naval warrant officer and neighbor;
   Kotaro Ishikawa, Yokosuka High School Principal;
   Isao Suzuki, the neighbor;
   Ginzo Kishi, whose son, Toshio, is now a town leader;
   Takataroh, the older brother;
   Kunka and Fugai Kato, the teacher and his brother;
   Yoshio Hirokawa, the fire chief.

   They are dead, every one.

   His Message. What is the true meaning of Yoshiharu's
message, inscribed on the back of the miniature photograph? Put the words together and what do they mean: spirit,
green, cool, wind, tempest, secret room, fragrance, light?

Perhaps Yoshiharu intended to make this simple announcement: "Yoshiharu Tsunoi was born of the Holy Spirit on July 7, 1938."

His love. Masuko would know the answers. She too, may have been a Christian.

His legacy. Peace. Religious freedom. These noble ideals eluded Yoshiharu to the end. He left no children, no fortune, no words of wisdom—only a symbol of his faith endures. But he is far from forgotten.

Hideo, Tatsuko, and Kiku remain alive. They cannot bring back the past. Those who know the truth are dead, leaving Yoshiharu's story unfinished.

I look out my porthole-shaped window and see shafts of light coming from the east, straight ahead of the Boeing. The ship hastens toward dawn. Presently, the rising sun embraces our aircraft in light and life. Passengers stir, stewardesses start down the aisles, and the pilot announces his slow downward descent toward British Columbia.

I have been awake all night. Yoshiharu's intriguing life—his conversion; his tragic end—these events remain shrouded, like mysteries unsolved.

It does not matter.

Yoshiharu has spoken. For now, he is not telling us any more.

Yoshiharu Tsunoi—*"Though dead, he speaks."*
(Courtesy of Tsunoi)

Yoshiharu (center) with unidentified group,
possibly including the Kato brothers, Kunka and Fugai
(Courtesy of Tsunoi)

Portrait of his grandmother, by Yoshiharu Tsunoi
(Courtesy of Tsunoi)

Epilogue

Upon hearing Yoshiharu's story, two people remarked, "Though dead he speaks,"—Bonnie Hansen of Parker, Colorado, and Reverend Claude Porter of Redding, California.

The phrase comes from Chapter 11 of the New Testament book of Hebrews, a dissertation on faith. This chapter describes men and women of antiquity who exhibited extraordinary trust in God. Their faith endured through

difficult times and uncertainties of life—persecution, preju-
dice, unfilled dreams, and ultimately, death.

Abel (Hebrews 11:4)—killed by his brother Cain in a
jealous rage—is named as one of those believers of long
ago.

In more recent history, we have encountered Yoshiharu.
He followed the example set before him, holding steadfast
to his faith during years of oppression. Caught and crushed
by war, Yoshiharu died clinging to his hopes and dreams.

This kind of faith can communicate over stretches of
time. Nothing can kill it—not sickness or health; tyranny
or benevolence; war or peace; time or distance; princi-
palities, powers, or created things. Not even death can still
the quiet voice of faith.

Postscript

We do not know how many Japanese flags, such as the one Yoshiharu carried, went to war—hundreds of thousands; perhaps a million. Most were destroyed on the battlefield. A few returned home with the soldiers who bore them. Others were spirited away by the victors. Many of these latter ones lie dormant, folded in chests or envelopes or boxes. Some will be uncovered by wives, sons, or daughters after their husband or father dies. The holders of these flags usually have no idea of their significance.

The flags can facilitate a vital closure between Japanese families and their dead. Yet, few have been returned to Japan.

Below is a listing of flags returned to Japan gratuitously since 1986, as compiled by the Sankai Press of Yokosuka. Only ten are cited. Although it may be incomplete, the list illustrates how slowly flags are being returned.

Returned 1986, May 20
Found on Luzon and taken to Florida. The governor of
Florida helped return it to Japan.

Returned 1986, August 14
Found on Iwajima.

Returned 1989, August 9
Found on Iwajima and taken to Houston, Texas.
Measures one meter by eighty centimeters.

Returned 1989, August 16
Found on Guadalcanal and taken to Wisconsin.

Returned 1989, December 1
Found on Negros, Philippines, by a twenty-five-year-old
soldier and taken to Texas.

Returned 1990, March 3.
Found on Marshall Islands.

Returned 1991, September 3
Found March 1945 on Leyte Island, Phillipines. Measures one meter by eighty centimeters with sixty-three
names inscribed. A professor from the University of Mei
went to New York and was given the flag by a veteran.
It had belonged to a twenty-four-year-old soldier and
was returned to his younger brother in Chiba, Japan.

Returned 1992, October 7
Found at Manila in 1945 by a twenty-six-year-old
soldier and taken to Washington state.

Returned 1992, December 8
Found on Guam in July 1944 and taken to California.
A Japanese exchange student found the flag in the home
where he was staying. The host, a veteran, did not know
what it was. It had belonged to a forty-three-year-old
commercial school teacher in Japan.

Returned 1995, August 11
Found at Cabcaben in February 1945 and taken to
California.
The Flag of Yoshiharu Tsunoi

If you have a flag you would like to return to Japan, the Japanese Consulate suggests contacting the Japan War Bereaved Families' Association. This group will locate the surviving family if possible.

Japan War Bereaved Families' Association
Nihon Izokukai
c/o Kudan Kaikan
1-6-5 Kudan-Minami
Chiyoda-Ku, Tokyo 102
Japan

Phone: 011-81-03-3261-5521
Fax: 011-81-03-3221-7237

Sources

Smith, Robert Ross (1963) - U.S. Army in WW11 - The War in the Pacific - Triumph in the Philippines: Washington, D.C., Office of Chief of Military History, 756pp.

Guthrie, B.D.,M.Th.,Ph.D. (1983) - The Letter to the Hebrews: Grand Rapids (MI), Inter-Varsity Press, 281pp.

Falk, Stanley Lawrence (1952) - The Bataan Death March: Georgetown University, MA thesis, 169pp.

Collier, Basil (1975) - Japan at War - An Illustrated History of the War in the Far East, 1931-1945: London, Sidwick & Jackson, 192pp.

Can any good thing arise
    From the ashes of Mount Samat—
That mosquito-plagued plot of land
    Stained with the blood of young men?

Behold, a small orphanage springing forth
    In that forgotten land of Bataan—
A beacon of life and love
    A salve to heal the wounded land.

    In 1994, an eighty-two-year-old American widow from the state of Washington started a good work near the slopes of Mount Samat.

King's Garden Children's Home
Orion, Philippines
Founded 1994 by
Lois Prater

"He who believes in Me, as the Scripture has said,
    Out of his heart will flow rivers of living water."
                                    John 7:38

Old photo of Mount Fuji
(Boisclaire collection)

船井義治君

ORDER FORM

Please send the following books by Yvonne Boisclaire:

*The Flag of Yoshiharu Tsunoi*_____ $8.95 each
*In the Shadow of the Rising Sun*_____ $15.95 each
(True story of an American POW, 1942-1945)

Price includes shipping for one book at book rate. Add $.75
       for each additional (may require up to three weeks).
For priority mail (3-5 days) add $2.00, one or two books.
International Air add $3.50, one or two books.

Add 7.25% sales tax for California address.
       ($.54 Yoshiharu, $1.05 Rising Sun)
Check here for autographed copy___
For personalized message, write on back of order form.

Name:_____

Address:_____

City_____State_____Zip_____

Check, money order, or Master Card/Visa accepted:
       Clearwood Publishers   Fax: 916-549-4598
       P.O. Box 52
       Bella Vista, CA 96008

Master/Card or Visa Number_____

Name on card:_____

Exp.date:_____Signature_____

ORDER FORM

Please send the following books by Yvonne Boisclaire:

_The Flag of Yoshiharu Tsunoi______ $8.95 each
_In the Shadow of the Rising Sun______ $15.95 each
(True story of an American POW, 1942-1945)

Price includes shipping for one book at book rate. Add $.75
        for each additional (may require up to three weeks).
For priority mail (3-5 days) add $2.00, one or two books.
International Air add $3.50, one or two books.

Add 7.25% sales tax for California address.
        ($.54 Yoshiharu, $1.05 Rising Sun)
Check here for autographed copy___
For personalized message, write on back of order form.

Name:_____

Address:_____

City_____State_____Zip_____

Check, money order, or Master Card/Visa accepted:
        Clearwood Publishers   Fax: 916-549-4598
        P.O. Box 52
        Bella Vista, CA 96008

Master/Card or Visa Number_____

Name on card:_____

Exp.date:_____Signature_____